Your guide to the

STRANGEST PUBS IN BRITAIN

- and the best worldwide -

FRONT COVER PICTURES

top left - Widow's Son - page 29

top right - The Crooked House - page 19

bottom left - The Pilchard Inn - page 23

bottom right - The Union Inn - page 38

STRANGEST
PUBS IN BRITAIN
- and the best worldwide -

TITLE NUMBER 1. FIRST EDITION.

WRITTEN & PUBLISHED BY
STRANGEST BOOKS

Published in England by Strangest Books (http://www.strangestbooks.co.uk).

ISBN 9780954320225

ACKNOWLEDGEMENTS

Thanks are given to those people who have kindly provided some of the photographs for inclusion in this book. These photographs are reproduced with the permission of the relevant copyright holders. Certain images appear from public domain.

This book is the result of extensive research and the entries contained herein are inserted at the sole discretion of the publishers. This does not indicate a preference over establishments not included. The publishers receive no payments or inducements for inclusion in this book.

foreword

Most of us can clearly remember a time when we saw or read about something that was so strange or unusual it made us gasp in wonder, or even sent a cold chill through our body.

The Strangest series of Books has the very best compilations of all that is weird, amazing and bizarre in Britain (and the rest of the world) today, and will open up a wonderland of curiosities for you to discover - most of which you probably never knew existed.

Each of the books in our series covers a chosen subject and will provide you with a thoroughly entertaining read. There are fascinating, mysterious, and very often unbelievable places and things to be seen. Some are so unusual that only a visit to actually see for yourself will suffice, or you can simply experience an unforgettable bedtime read, and then amaze your friends and colleagues with some of the startling facts.

Sure to provide readers with as much pleasure as they did for the researchers, the Strangest series of Books can be purchased or ordered from all good book stores and high street retailers. Information on how to order direct can be found on page 96.

Outside of a dog,

a book is a man's best friend.

Inside of a dog, its too dark to read.

- Groucho Marx

about this book

With well over 60,000 to choose from, the abundance and diversity of pubs in Britain is truly superb and it is little wonder that in this respect we are envied worldwide.

Widely acclaimed by numerous celebrities and the media, Strangest Pubs in Britain *and the best worldwide* is a rollercoaster ride of amazement, and this book is dedicated to providing readers with tales of the weirdest and wackiest pubs there are. Read all about where you must leave your shoe as a deposit for a drink, the amazing Crooked House where your drink slides up the table, or the pub where you play skittles with a block of cheese. A door layered with human skin, a pub shaped and constructed like a pack of cards, or how would you like to have a drink in the underwater bar?

Find out where there is a pub made out of ice, the smallest, oldest and most remote pubs, and much more. From the bizarre and eccentric pubs, to the weird and downright crazy pubs, they are all here in a book you will want to read more than once - Strangest Pubs in Britain *and the best worldwide.*

alphabetical index of entries

Part One - BRITAIN

Part Two - USA

Part Three - REST OF WORLD

Part One
- BRITAIN -

The Crooked House - page 19.

THE FROG & TOAD
38 Burnt Oak Terrace, Gillingham, Kent

Popular and worth visiting for more than one unusual reason, The Frog & Toad pub in Gillingham sells a huge range of Belgian beers, but it is one type in particular that will leave you 'legless' - or more specifically, shoeless.

The tradition in Belgium if you want to buy the 8% 'Kwak' ale is that you leave one of your shoes as a deposit, to prevent souvenir hunters running off with the elaborate glass and wooden frame it is served in. The glass is shaped like a miniature yard of ale glass and as it will not rest on the counter it is supported in an ornamental wooden frame - complete with handle - with the combination costing about £5 each to manufacture.

The Frog & Toad have taken the idea one step further and have six ropes behind the bar which run over the ceiling of the bar to the customers side and are attached to wire baskets. The customer (by now bemused) is asked to deposit his shoe in the basket which is in turn hoisted up to the ceiling, remaining there until the return of the glass and frame.

Unscrupulous patrons who deposit a shoe that is obviously on its last legs will be politely requested to stick a £5 note inside as an added security! Big attractive thermal slipper socks are offered to customers who suffer from 'cold feet', and these are washed together with the bar towels which gives a whole new meaning to smelly feet.

Equally wacky is the inspirational idea of snail racing, and the team who were responsible for the Guinness television advert hosted one such event at The Frog & Toad. It was a huge success, has been held again, and looks set to become the annual World Championships.

There were 10 snails in each race all of which had a number attached to their shell. Racing on a damp cloth from a small inner circle to a larger outer circle, the first across the outside line was the winner. Customers backed their favourite snail and, thoughtfully, all profits were donated to good causes.

Snails and slugs are gastropods which make up the largest class of molluscs with over 60,000 species. Snails move about by sliding on their single foot which has a specialised gland to secrete mucus. This lubricates the path over which the snails crawl. Freshwater snails and land snails have always been eaten by people and they are a delicacy in many countries.

A previous Guinness Gastropod Championship held in central London featured an attempt to break the world 13 inch sprinting record which was held by 'Archie' at an incredible 2 minutes and 20 seconds. This equates to a speed of 0.0085 kilometres per hour although it is said that snails have been measured at speeds of 0.048 kilometres per hour.

Depositing a shoe for 'Kwak' ale, and (below) not quite a sprint finish with snail racing.

SOMERSET HOUSE
121 Enville Street, Stourbridge, West Midlands

Who would have believed it? Somerset House, the subject of various television, radio and newspaper reports, hit the headlines as a pub where you can park your pint unsupported on its walls!
With a sceptical mind (and a lunchtime thirst) we went along to investigate, and came away as bemused as the German camera crew who had preceded us. The phenomenon has been probed by scientists who arrived at the conclusion that the wallpaper glue was responsible. Their assumption is based on a suspicion that a combination of glue, old tobacco smoke and grime is enough to hold a full pint against the wall, sometimes for a day or more, although they admit it is very odd.

Regulars at Somerset House are not convinced however and believe the walls are magic, whilst others insist the pub is haunted. Spookily enough coffins used to be assembled on this land just out the back and tales abound of mysterious happenings over the years.

What is beyond dispute is the fact that the picture below was taken by our own photographer at this unassuming West Midlands local and clearly shows his pint suspended unaided from the wall of the pub. Minutes later it was drank, and very welcome it was too. Although the pub has since been redecorated your drink will still hang ‘magically’ from its walls.

- built like a pack of cards -

PACK O'CARDS
High Street, Combe Martin, Devon

A remarkable pub which is a magnet for tourists, this was built by the village squire in 1690 with the winnings from a card game as a tribute to 'Lady Luck'.

Constructed to resemble a deck of cards, it was built on a plot of land measuring 52ft x 52ft, has 4 floors (representing the number of suits in a pack), 13 doors on every floor and 13 fireplaces (number of cards in a suit), 52 stairs (number of cards in a pack), and prior to window tax the panes of glass in all the windows added up to the total of the numbered cards in a pack. Must be seen.

HAUNCH OF VENISON
Salisbury, Wiltshire

This was built as the church house for nearby St.Thomas's. In addition to a 600 year old fireplace this ancient old building has a glass covered slit in the wall, behind which is a smoke preserved, mummified hand of a most unfortunate 18th century card player.

GEORGE & DRAGON INN
High Street, Potterne, near Devizes, Wiltshire

The village of Potterne is mentioned in the Domesday Book, and located in the village is the George & Dragon Inn which has a tunnel leading to a pub in the next village. It is known that this tunnel was used by Oliver Cromwell.

A unique .22 shooting gallery is housed within the pub - believed to be the only one located in a pub in the world - and regular competitions are held here every Thursday evening. Marksmen shoot along a metal tube from a hatch into the target area housed in an adjacent small building. New participants are always welcome and frequent open nights are held.

Incredibly, the whole thing was started here over 100 years ago in 1906 by a member of royalty.

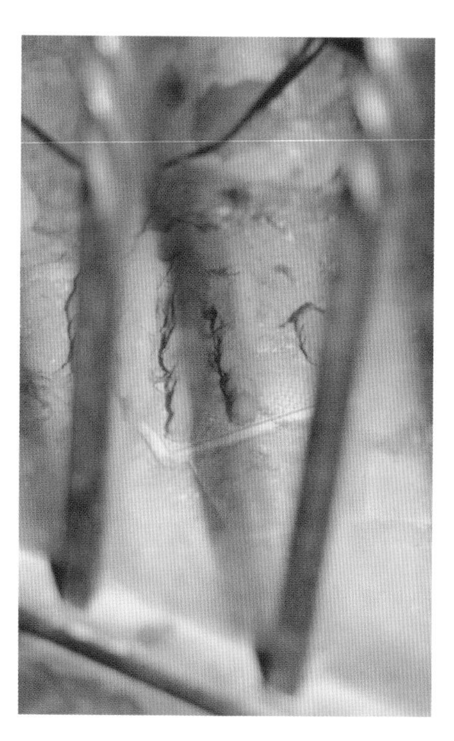

The mummified digits of an ill-fated 18th century card player that can be seen at the Haunch of Venison. Perhaps he played one hand too many.

THE CROOKED HOUSE
Coppice Mill, Himley, near Dudley, Staffordshire

This typical 'black country' pub was built as a farmhouse in 1765 and is one of the country's best public house attractions - as a pub that really is crooked. It was originally known as 'The Glynne Arms' as it was named after Sir Stephen Glynne on whose estate the pub stood.

The pub is now 4ft lower on one side than on the other due to subsidence from the effects of coal mining during the 1800's, and it is heavily supported with buttresses and girders.

The amazing angle that the pub sits at has to be seen to be believed.
In fact The Crooked House is one huge optical illusion where curtains hang away from the window frames, marbles roll uphill on the wall beading, and drinks slide slowly 'up table'. It is also allegedly haunted.

SEVERNSHED RESTAURANT & BAR
Harbourside, The Grove, Bristol

Housed in a former boathouse that was built in 1843 by renowned engineer Isambard Kingdom Brunel, is the astonishing Severnshed Restaurant and bar - astonishing because of the fact that it has one of the greatest innovations of modern times; a 6 ton 'floating' steel bar that can rotate 360 degrees and glide up and down the length of the building on hover pads.

THE HATCHET INN

27 Frogmore Street,
Bristol

Once the haunt of notorious highwaymen, The Hatchet Inn is Bristol's oldest public house and was established in 1606. The 400 year old main door of the pub is said to have layers of human skin under the tar and many large offers have been made for it, but all declined.

A cockfighting ring and a boxing ring have been here, and bare knuckle fights involving 'All England Champions' attracted enormous purses in days gone by.

The 400 year old front door (left) of the Hatchet Inn pub, reputed to have layers of human skin under the tar coating.

TREVOR ARMS HOTEL
Marford Village, Wrexham, Clwyd, North Wales

Marford is an amazing village full of buildings that ooze character and the odd thing is that most of the buildings, including The Trevor Arms Hotel which dates back to the early 1800's, feature a cross, or crosses, which are intended to ward off evil spirits. In fact The Trevor Arms Hotel has 4 or 5 of these set into its structure.

The story relates that following a battle in Paris between Catholics and Protestants in the late 1700's, which the Catholics won, the Protestants made their escape up the River Seine and eventually - via the River Dee - landed at Ecclestone Ferry nearby.

Marford Village is built in a Dutch style, with a place in Holland believed to be identical. There is little doubt that the buildings and their unusual architecture, with even more striking windows and strange crosses, are the work of these Europeans.

The rear of the Trevor Arms Hotel with crosses hewn into the stonework of the structure.

An unusual dwelling with strange windows and carved crosses in the village of Marford.

THE PILCHARD INN

Burgh Island, Bigbury on Sea, Devon

This famous 14th century white walled pub is located on a small tidal island and can only be reached - when the tide is in - by enjoying a ride on a giant sea-tractor. At other times visitors can walk across the sandy causeway. Pirates and smugglers once used the island as a base as the tides and currents made it secure. The famous writer Agatha Christie was a regular visitor here. Burgh Island lies several hundred yards off the coast at Bigbury on Sea and was even commandeered by the Army during the Second World War due to its strategic importance.

NEW INN

Blists Hill Open Air Museum, Ironbridge, Telford, Shropshire

The New Inn is actually a reconstructed 19th century public house from Green Lane, Walsall, and was opened for business at Blists Hill Open Air Museum in March 1983. A number of potential pubs were considered before this was selected and then moved brick by brick (as with many of the other buildings here) to its present location.

The scrubbed wood and sawdust covered floors appear very much as they would have done many years ago, and a pewter measure of 'mother's ruin' can be bought for about 3d (3 pence in old money prior to decimilisation). You can change sterling into this old currency at the local bank on site and it can be spent at the bakery, chemist, and a host of other attractions.

Staff at the pub wear authentic period dress and it is startling to see this former predominantly male preserve, with many original parts, as it would have appeared in the intervening years since its original construction about 1880.

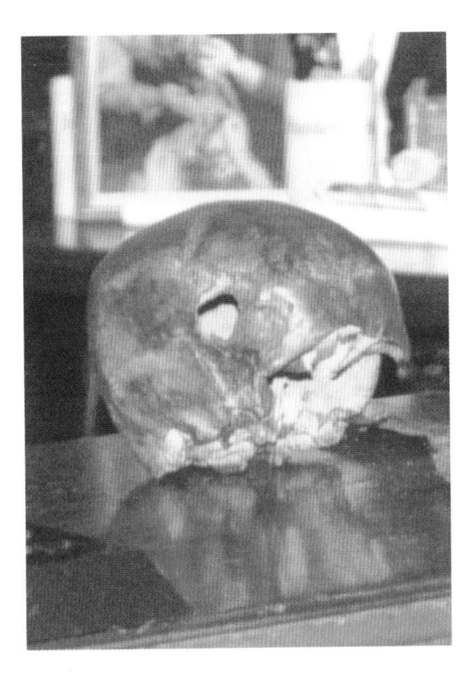

JORROCKS
41 Iron Gate, Derby, Derbyshire

Previously called The George, and also D.Lafferty & Son, this was built around 1693. There are many strange tales surrounding this pub and it was once the most famous coaching inn in Derby.

The 'George Skull' on display in the pub is a female human skull that has a damaged cranium. It was discovered by workmen in a pit below the cellar floor together with animal bones and skulls, plus old shoes and pieces of leather. Forensic tests at Nottingham indicated a great age, and the mystery is how - or why - only the skull and not the rest of the skeleton came to be in the pit.

As Jorrocks stands near the corner of Iron Gate (where blacksmiths traded) and Sadler Gate (where leather workers traded) which is the heart of Viking Derby, it can perhaps explain how the pieces of leather were discovered as it was usual for the leather makers to throw any offcuts into a pit after the hides had been stripped and tanned. An explanation for the animal bones and skulls may be that they were from animals killed for the leather makers. The enigma of the human skull and the damage to the side of it remains unsolved.

The pub is undoubtedly haunted as on a few occasions a long haired man in a blue coat has been seen walking along the landing in the middle of the night. When followed down to the bar he has simply disappeared, although there was nowhere for him to go. Staff have reported many odd experiences since the building work and extension of the cellar has been completed including buckets being thrown, crockery moving by itself, pint pots smashed, and ghastly groans emanating from the cellar.

There is also said to be a ghost named Martha who frequently insists that her head (the 'George Skull') be taken from the bar and reburied.

As the mysteries surrounding the skull continues to baffle all who seek the answers we can only wonder; was she murdered and if so why? Where is the rest of her skeleton? Is she the ghostly presence behind all the strange happenings at the pub? What is known is that 2 murders have actually taken place in the adjoining alley.

GEORGE & DRAGON
High Street, Cley-next-the-Sea, Norfolk

Dedicated to bird-watching of the feathered kind, the George & Dragon is the ideal place for 'twitchers' to pursue their hobby. Cley Marshes Nature Reserve has resident herons, wagtails, hawks, grebes and woodpeckers, in addition to visiting cormorants, puffins and razorbills, etc.

This imposing building has its own 'hide' where watchers can observe some of the rare species. One bedroom/hide room can be reserved (with binoculars supplied free of charge), and a separate room is for general observation by twitchers.

A 'Bird Bible' (or diary) is located on a lectern and contains many illustrations by famous bird watchers. It is updated on a daily basis and provides watchers with a wealth of information.

THE STAR INN
Manor Road, Sulgrave, near Banbury, Northamptonshire

There are plenty of curios and oddities in this former farmhouse to keep your attention for a week. The most bizarre must be the many newspaper front pages on display that have headlines screaming out such things as the first hole in the heart operation, Kennedy's assassination, and the death of Churchill.

Weird stuffed animals include a hare's head with small antlers fitted to make it resemble a tiny stag, the backside of a fox appearing to jump through the wall, and a kangaroo with a hanging-corks hat. They certainly make you stop and think. A blackboard usually displays a weird and obscure fact of the day.

THE LITTLE DRY DOCK

Windmill End, Netherton, near Dudley, West Midlands

Built as a barge-station for boats going up the Netherton Tunnel to New Street Station, this was turned into a pub shortly after the war - with a complete narrowboat still inside, which is now actually the bar. The pub is full of barge memorabilia and is located below an impressive junction of the canal network.

Opposing views of a bar that is actually a barge.

Old buns and fresh buns at the Widow's Son in East London.

WIDOW'S SON
75 Devon's Road, Bow, London E3

A sad tale accompanies the curiously named Widow's Son in East London. Prior to it becoming a pub a poor widow lived in a cottage on this site about 200 years ago. Her only son was a sailor, and as he was due to return home from sea one Good Friday his mother baked him some hot-cross buns. Unfortunately he never returned home and nothing was heard of him again, but his mother continued to have a new bun waiting for him every Good Friday thereafter - which was subsequently added to the buns she had kept from previous years. When she died the buns were discovered hanging from a beam in her cottage. The house thereafter became known to locals as 'Bun House' and, although it was eventually replaced by a pub around 1848, this delightful story and tradition was continued by successive landlords.

Every Good Friday a Royal Navy sailor arrives to present a new bun which is added to the mouldy shrunken collection that hangs over the bar, and today, sailors from all parts of the country call in from time to time to pay their respects to the widow - in addition to having a good time at this plain and unassuming East London pub.

THE BELL INN
High Road, Horndon-On-The-Hill, Stanford-Le-Hope, Essex

A similar, although not a tragic story, concerns the attractive timber beamed bar at the medieval 15th century Bell Inn in Essex. They too have an odd collection of hot-cross buns hanging from their heavy beams. The story here is that the pub was taken over on Good Friday of 1903 by Jack Turnell, who celebrated the occasion by hanging a hot cross bun from the timbers.

The tradition has been kept going ever since and even during the war when food was scarce, a concrete bun was hung instead! Nowadays the oldest person available at the time has the honour of hanging the annual bun every Easter at The Bell Inn.

The curious collection of buns at The Bell Inn.

The Chequered Skipper. Not a pub to get hammered in.

THE CHEQUERED SKIPPER

The Green, Ashton Oundle, Peterborough, Cambridgeshire

This is probably the most unique pub sign in the country. Full size, it depicts a colourful butterfly and is made completely out of many different types of nails.

FOX & HOUNDS

High Street, Barley, Royston, Hertfordshire

The Fox & Hounds at Barley has a famous and very rare gallows pub sign which is a beam that traverses the road. The carvings are superb in a depiction of a hunting scene that has a fox being chased by 2 huntsmen on horseback and a pack of dogs.

The origins of pub and inn signs can be traced back to the Romans when vine leaves were displayed to indicate that they sold wine. Subsequently, in Britain small evergreen bushes were used.

As the naming of inns and alehouses became popular by the 12th century, signs were also added. This was common practice as most of the population could neither read nor write. In 1393 an Act was passed making it compulsory for a sign to be displayed for identification purposes.

Before the Reformation many inn signs followed a religious theme, but when Henry split with the Catholic church numerous King's Heads and Crown's became popular as signs.

The Victorian era saw much competition for trade as countless 'gin palaces' sprang up. As interiors became more extravagant the inn signs followed suit. Signs got so large and imposing that eventually there were ordinances against them as they were considered dangerous. Very few of these colossal gallows signs exist today.

TAN HILL INN
Richmond, Tan Hill, Yorkshire

This isolated old stone pub is Britain's highest at 1,732ft above sea level. It is located on the border of North Yorkshire and Durham, also close to the border with Cumbria, and it often becomes snowbound during winter.

PLOUGH
Great Munden, near Ware, Hertfordshire

The largest musical instrument in any pub in the country is the full size working Compton theatre organ that can be seen (and heard) in the specially built extension at the Plough.

THE VICTORIA INN
88 Victoria Road, Swindon, Wiltshire

Film buffs who would enjoy a good movie that much more with a pint of real ale in hand should head for The Victoria Inn. The pub has soundproofed its Dungeon Bar and created a cinema that can hold around 35 people. Regular weekly showings that include the latest releases means visitors can view most films earlier than the satellite channels show them.

The films are shown with a DVD and a £12,000 stereo sound system. It is believed to be the first pub in Britain to be granted special film and music licences from the Performing Rights Society, the video broadcasting authorities, and Swindon Borough Council. Choc-ices anyone?

THE GREEN MAN
Harrods Department Store, Knightsbridge, London W1

The Green Man is unusual in that it is a pub in a department store, but not any old department store. It is situated in the famous Harrods store in Knightsbridge London, and is a superb period style traditional pub with an eye-catching gilded ceiling and delicately carved wood features.

THE BLIND BEGGAR
337 Whitechapel Road, Spitalfields, London E1

Located near where the notorious Jack the Ripper murder attrocities occurred, The Blind Beggar could possibly be described as Britain's most notorious pub. Although now a very pleasant establishment, on March 8th of 1966 George Cornell of the infamous Richardson gang was drinking in The Blind Beggar when Ronald Kray - one of the Kray twins - walked into the bar and shot him dead through the head.

ELEPHANTS NEST
Horndon, Marytavy, Tavistock, Devon

This unspoilt 400 year old pub has its name written on the beams in about 60 different languages - all done by a succession of different visitors, and even some by old landlords.

THE ARCTIC BAR
3-5 New Entry, Dundee, Scotland

This is one of the oldest pubs in the area and the name 'Arctic Bar' is believed to have originated from the whalers who used to call in and collect their wages at the bar. In keeping with its name, one of the most prominent features is a depiction in the floor of the bar showing a polar bear on top of an iceberg.

There are 6 doors in the bar area that each have coffin shaped windows, probably installed in memory of 6 local whalers who were lost at sea. Whaling once formed a major part of the economy in this part of Scotland and old unused whaling stations can still be seen today.

THE PILLARS
9 & 15 Crichton Street, Dundee, Scotland

This late 18th century building has a model of the Old Town House - which was affectionately known as 'The Pillars' - located over the main entrance door.

Unusual is the fact that the bar entrance is at number 9 Crichton Street whilst the lounge entrance is located at number 15 Crichton Street. They are connected by the upper lounge to the rear of the building, with a Driving School below them in the middle!

The building dates from a time when Crichton Street was the first of many streets to be cut through from the High Street to the River Tay, thus creating the very first non-medieval passage to the waterfront.

THE NILE
9-21 Castle Street, Inverness, Highlands, Scotland

For a taste of Egypt visit the Scottish Highlands. This is not as crazy as it sounds as The Nile bar in Inverness is a superb Egyptian orientated experience where visitors can see an entire bar front resembling carved out sandstone blocks, a sarcophagus, and numerous hieroglyphics. The pictures on the walls of old Egyptians remind you of a Cairo bazaar and there is certainly no other place in Scotland quite like this. The phrase 'walk like an Egyptian' could well have originated here after one too many.

THE DROVERS INN
Inverarnan, Loch Lomond, Scotland

Visitors are sure to have the feeling that, externally, The Drovers Arms has remained untouched for decades, and this feeling will certainly prevail when entering the pub. You are greeted at the entrance hall by the outstretched arms of a stuffed grizzly bear standing on its hind legs, whilst multiple stuffed birds and small animals stare at you with beady eyes from glass fronted display cabinets. The overall impression is one of timelessness and the bar area is little different. Apart from welcoming fires it has a stuffed golden eagle to admire perched at the end of it. All of this is greatly enhanced by staff in traditional kilts and sometimes piped Scottish music that welcomes all visitors, including many climbers and walkers.

Jekyll & Hyde pub.

JEKYLL & HYDE PUB
112 Hanover Street, Edinburgh, Scotland

The Jekyll & Hyde pub is one of many that are in some way connected with - or based on - characters created by Scotland's most famous literary son, Robert Louis Stevenson. Horror movies play constantly at the pub, and the toilets are hidden behind bookcases!

The unforgettable Jekyll and Hyde have long been immortalised in motion pictures. The Strange Case of Dr Jekyll and Mr Hyde was penned by Stevenson following his marriage to Fanny Osborne in 1878, together with other classics he wrote such as Treasure Island and Kidnapped. It was Deacon William Brodie (see Deacon Brodies below) who provided the inspiration for Jekyll and Hyde, courtesy of his bizarre double-life. Born into a famous Edinburgh engineering family, Stevenson was dogged by ill health. He died in Samoa in 1894 but left a legacy of literary genius and was much beloved.

DEACON BRODIES
435 Lawnmarket, Edinburgh, Scotland

A cabinet-maker and respected councillor by day, Brodie was a burglar by night. An armed raid on His Majesty's Excise Office proved his downfall and he was hanged in 1788, ironically from a gibbet he had recently redesigned. Robert Louis Stevenson's father had cabinets made by Brodie, and Stevenson used Brodie's split personality as the basis for a book.

HAWES INN
Newhalls Road, South Queensferry, near Edinburgh, West Lothian, Scotland

The novel 'Kidnapped' was started here by Robert Louis Stevenson in room 13. The Hawes Inn has one of the most striking locations of any pub in the country - in the shadow of the immense Forth road and rail bridges.

Dinner doing the 100 metres at The Barley Mow.

THE BARLEY MOW

The Dale, Bonsall, Matlock, Derbyshire

The Barley Mow at Bonsall has held its world famous 'Chicken Races' for about 20 years. On the first Saturday in August a 20 metre marked track on the car park is transformed into a feather-flying battle of the fittest hens around. There have been rumours that hen racing has been held in the area for decades and The Barley Mow is said to be carrying on that tradition.

Strict rules are in place here as birds must start with their feet on the ground (no air launched hens allowed), cockerels and dogs are barred for the day, and violence is strictly prohibited as hen-pecking can lead to a suspension.

The event is extremely popular, with large crowds always in attendance to witness this annual 'chicken olympics' spectacle.

The village of Bonsall has made the headlines many times regarding numerous mysterious UFO sightings in the area. Around 20 sightings were reported during one month alone including one by a lady that was actually recorded on camcorder. It was said in the local newspaper that she was paid a figure of £20,000 by a television company for exclusive rights to the footage which showed an unidentified craft hovering over fields near her home.

The area in general is a hotbed for UFO sightings and a constant stream of visitors from all over the country call in at The Barley Mow public house to join the landlord's tours - in the hope of witnessing an extraterrestrial occurrence themselves.

Many villagers are said to have experienced these unexplained sightings but some are reluctant to talk about them. The pub landlord patiently and frequently spends time with visitors to The Barley Mow discussing the sightings and informing them of the best reported locations to visit.

There is no doubt that something is afoot at Bonsall and it is hoped that either further investigations, or future irrefutable evidence, may yet reveal that we are not alone.

CROWS NEST
Crows Nest, Darite, Cornwall

This was formerly the pay office and company store where local tin miners were paid. Apart from the obvious memorabilia connected with the tin mining industry there is also a highly unusual table which was converted from a huge blacksmith's bellows. Incidentally the bellows still work.

COBWEB INN
Penhally Hill, Boscastle, Cornwall

This is one of the most interesting pubs in Cornwall and at one time it had huge cobwebs throughout the building that were occupied by massive spiders. It is said that neither the staff nor customers were permitted to destroy a cobweb or there would be big trouble.

The pub is of course much more pleasant nowadays and some of its current unusual features are the large collection of hundreds of colourful old bottles hanging from the beams in the bar, and an enormous armchair that has been completely carved out of a treetrunk.

THE CRAB & LOBSTER
Disforth Road, Asenby, near Thirsk, Yorkshire

The Crab & Lobster has an abundance of odd curiosities on display. There is also an interesting array of seating that includes settees, antique high-backed chairs, theatrical corner seats, and even a dentist's chair!

OLDE BULLS HEAD
Castle Street, Beaumaris, Anglesey, North Wales

On display at the Olde Bulls Head in Beaumaris is the town's old ducking stool and some fearsome looking cutlasses. The pub however is most famous for the gigantic courtyard door which is the largest single-hinged door in Britain.

THE WHITE SWAN
34 Frenchgate, Doncaster, Yorkshire

The small front room type bar at the White Swan has, reputedly, the tallest bar in Britain at about 5ft in height. Stiletto shoes help here then.

THE MALTINGS
Tanners Moat, York, Yorkshire

The front of the bar and the entire ceiling of The Maltings is completely made from doors.

GEORGE HOTEL
Land Of Green Ginger, Hull, Humberside

This former Elizabethan mansion has 4 intriguing mysteries that visitors may care to solve, as well as what is probably the smallest window in England that measures just half an inch wide by 13 inches in length.

Depicting Roman life (above) and (below) close up view of Roman Bath.

THE ROMAN BATH
St.Sampson's Square, York, Yorkshire

Hidden away for 2,000 years, the famous well preserved Roman Bath in the basement of this pub was discovered in 1930 when the pub was enlarged. It is now illuminated, open to the public, and visitors can enjoy the experience from a specially constructed viewing platform.

The pub itself also has superb depictions of Roman times running the length of its walls and no visit to York - one of the most important Roman historical cities in the country - would be complete without a visit to The Roman Bath.

Baths have been part of Roman life since the 2nd century BC and were initially for men only. These were the places where important matters and business were discussed. By 33 BC it is estimated there were almost 200 baths (both private and public) in Rome alone, and as the Roman empire grew so did the number of bathing places - which became more and more luxurious. By the end of the 4th century AD there were over 1,000 baths in Rome including huge public baths such as the Diocletian which could easily cater for 3,000 bathers. A slave would be taken along by the wealthy to hold towels, oils, and other bathing requisites. The Tepidarium (warm room) was the forerunner of our modern day sauna, and this would be used - sometimes with the services of a masseur - before using the main baths.

Viewing platform at the Roman Bath.

THE UNION INN

Tamar Street, Waterside, Saltash, Cornwall

The Union Inn can be found on the historic Waterside at Saltash, impressively positioned to the western side of the River Tamar which forms the boundary line between Devon and Cornwall. It lies in the shadows of 2 gigantic bridges; the Tamar Suspension Bridge opened in 1961 to meet the growing demand of motorists, and the Prince Albert Railway Bridge designed by Isambard Kingdom Brunel and opened in 1859.

Equally as dominating a sight as the bridges, The Union Inn has a striking Union Jack painted and emblazoned over the whole of the front of the pub. It is recorded as having been painted in 1995 to mark the 50th anniversary of V.E.Day, and not for attention-seeking reasons - although it no doubt draws many a backward glance from those crossing the river by car or rail.

The entire east wall of the pub is taken up with a gigantic mural instigated by former Saltash Mayor Peter Stephens, and painted by local artist David Whitley over the course of 3 months. It depicts Saltash through the ages and includes old customers alongside more famous faces such as Sir Francis Drake and Isambard Kingdom Brunel.

Pictures inside The Union Inn depict the colourful history of the Waterside and how times have changed since the turn of the century. Roundheads and Cavaliers previously fought over Saltash in a series of bloody encounters with one battle alone reputed to have claimed over 700 lives, right here at the Waterside.

Although some may describe it as mildly eccentric, the pub is a hive of activity and does much to support local good causes.

PUFF INN
St.Kilda, Outer Hebrides, Scotland

The archipeligo of St.Kilda found approximately 41 miles (66 kilometres) west of Benbecula in Scotland's Outer Hebrides consists of Hirta, Soay, Boreray and Dun, and they are collectively known as 'the islands at the edge of the world'. 'Kilda' is probably a corruption of the Norse word 'skildir', as there has never been a St. or Saint Kilda. There have been people on St.Kilda since Prehistoric times, and stone tools discovered on Hirta indicate that Bronze Age travellers may have visited from the Western Isles up to 5,000 years ago. St.Kilda society existed virtually isolated from all others for well over 1,000 years until increasing contact with the mainland eventually brought about its downfall. Missionaries and tourists inevitably brought along with them the money orientated values of the mainland, in addition to diseases. In 1930 the islanders, who could no longer support themselves, were voluntarily evacuated. A small group emigrated to Australia, and even today a suburb of the city of Melbourne is called St.Kilda (there is also a St.Kilda in New Zealand).

In 1931 the islands were sold to a keen ornithologist, the 5th Marquess of Bute, who subsequently bequeathed them to the National Trust for Scotland in 1957. Due to its importance, in 1986 St.Kilda was designated a natural World Heritage Site. The exceptional cliffs which are the highest in Britain form the premier seabird breeding station in Europe, and the world's largest colony of gannets nests on Boreray. The St.Kildans used to eat seabirds as a major part of their diet with Puffin in particular being very popular.

Left on the islands is one of the most extensive groups of vernacular building remains to be found anywhere in Britain. The whole layout of the 19th century village remains can be seen to this day and there are over 1,400 stone cleitean (used for storing fuel and food) scattered all over the islands.

A small area of land on Hirta has been in use (on renewable 25 year leases) as a radar tracking station for the missile range located on Benbecula in the Outer Hebrides. St.Kilda attracts all sorts of people, in all kinds of weather, and in all types of craft.

Incredibly there is a pub on St.Kilda. The Puff Inn is the most remote pub in Britain being some 50 miles out in the Atlantic from Lewis in the Outer Hebrides. It is operated by Serco, who run a lot of the Army facilities in Britain, and caters for a resident population of 35 or so Army, conservation volunteers and wardens, sheep minders, and visiting boats. It is a proper pub with liberal opening hours where anyone can get a drink, although being accessible only 3 months a year by boat, or at other times by helicopter from Benbecula, you can hardly make it your new local.

THE OLD FORGE
Inverie, Knoydart, Mallaig, Inverness'shire, Scotland

The Old Forge is the most remote pub on mainland Britain, as confirmed by the Guinness Book of Records.

THE FARMHOUSE
St.Isidore's Road, Grange Farm, Kesgrave, Suffolk

The word of God is administered to pub-goers in this Suffolk village inn by a Reverend from the local All Saints Church. Parishioners have welcomed the idea which was started towards the end of 2001 and is now a regular monthly occurrence. The first service was held in conjunction with a simultaneous service at the 900 year old All Saints Church; the service ending abruptly when the pub opened its doors at noon.

The vicar believes the services will help diminish the staid image that people have of them, and all denominations in the parish believe it is a great idea. The pub is now affectionately known as 'All Saints Farmhouse Community Pub'.

THE CROWN INN
Ramsgate Road, Sarre, near Birchington, Kent

There has been an inn on this site since about 1500 and this Grade I Listed building previously played host to the many reunion dinners of the survivors of the famous Charge of the Light Brigade. It is known locally as the 'Cherry Brandy House' and the recipe for this drink was brought over by the Huguenots (French Protestants) who were fleeing from the religious persecutions of Louis XIV. It is believed that one of them bought the ale house at Sarre (which is now The Crown Inn) and started to produce the cherry brandy after being reminded of his family recipe when seeing fruit orchards in the area.

A requirement of subsequent licensees was that the liqueur be permanently available and, today, the cherry brandy whose secret recipe is zealously guarded is sold exclusively at The Crown Inn and nowhere else in the world.

THE SCOTSMAN PACK INN
School Lane, Hathersage, Hope Valley, Derbyshire

'Little John' was a giant whose body now lies in a grave at a Hathersage graveyard. A chair which was specially constructed for him can be seen at The Scotsman Pack Inn. It is affectionately known as 'Little John's Chair' and was won in a wager by a Major John J. Lewis of the Manchester Regiment in 1950.

It is known that the chair was at the pub during the 1920's and 1930's, although it then went missing for a while, but was presented back to the pub by a Mrs M. Lucas in 1960. The immense chair is a rare sight indeed.

RED LION HOTEL
1 Old Hall Street, Malpas, Cheshire

The chair King James I used is still here and a tradition states that if you sit in the chair you must pay a penny for the privilege, or pay for a round of drinks for everyone.

WAXY O'CONNORS
14-16 Rupert Street, London W1

The labyrinth of individually designed interconnecting rooms, bars and alcoves at Waxy O'Connors makes this the drinking experience of a lifetime. Gothic, Celtic, and awe-inspiring are words that readily spring to mind when attempting to describe this 9,000 square foot pub.

Entering at street level you then descend to other levels, and the many areas include the Cottage Room, the spectacular Church Bar complete with wood carvings, pulpit, confessional box and gargoyles, and the Tree Room - which features a massive 250 year old beech tree from the Midlands in Ireland, 'growing' from floor to ceiling through 2 storeys. A church from Ireland was actually taken down, transported here and rebuilt.

Wherever you sit or stand at Waxy O'Connors there is a stunning feature to be admired, and the lower level Dargle restaurant is no exception.

Enormous Irish beech tree growing through 2 storeys of Waxy O'Connors.

THE CANAL HOUSE
Canal Street, Nottingham, Nottinghamshire

This converted industrial building has a very striking feature - there is actually a canal running through the bar! Visitors will quite often see a boat moored up there as well, so if you are on a boating holiday by canal in Nottingham and want to quench your thirst, why not cruise in.

THE BARGE INN

Honey Street, near Pewsey, Wiltshire

The frequent new discoveries and overall enigma of crop circles receives constant press coverage and in the heart of the Vale of Pewsey lies a pub that is very much a part of this unexplained phenomena.

From late spring each year The Barge Inn becomes the centre of attention for thousands of visitors from all over the world who are keen to discover the latest on crop circles, and perhaps witness the most recent of these stunning designs to appear.

Crop circles are by no means a modern phenomenon. About 200 cases were reported prior to 1970 and they are even mentioned in academic texts of the late 17th century. The mystery is who or what created them.

From simple designs such as circles, or circles with rings, they then developed lines. Today they have evolved into breathtaking pictograms with many displaying amazing computer fractals and elements that could only be found in quantum physics processes. The sizes of these stunning creations have also greatly increased with some reported as covering areas of 150,000 - 250,000 sq ft. They generally appear overnight and the sheer complexity of them dismisses the notion that they could possibly be man-made. Hoaxing inevitably occurs frequently but there can be no explanation for the detection of high levels of energy, background radiation, infrared output, and electromagnetism associated with them. It is reported that in 1996 a pilot flew over Stonehenge and saw nothing unusual, but on flying back over the monument 15 minutes later an immense 600 ft series of crop circles had appeared, resembling the Julia Set computer fractal, and comprising of 149 circles.

It is little wonder then that The Barge Inn near Pewsey in Wiltshire has become a mecca for crop circle enthusiasts, being located in a county renowned for numerous sightings. In fact parts of the inn more resemble a research lab than a pub. Giant noticeboards in the pubs 'Crop Room' keep visitors up to date and there are numerous photographs, letters and diagrams everywhere. A huge map covered with coloured stickers details past and present crop circle sightings and the manager has transformed the place into a focal point for the curious hordes who descend on the pub each year.

On the ceiling of the 'Crop Room' is a large impressive mural that depicts the ancient monuments of Wiltshire - Stonehenge, Silbury Hill, Avebury and the White Horse. All are linked together with circles, swirls, and other symbols that have been spotted in local cornfields. The mural was painted by ex-local artist Vince Palmer.

The 'croppies' and professional researchers who visit The Barge Inn are kept well up to date with all local sightings and enthusiasts range from teenagers to the elderly.

Whoever or whatever the reasons behind these beautiful formations, The Barge Inn stands a good chance of being the first to know when that discovery is made.

YE OLDE TRIP TO JERUSALEM

1 Brewhouse Yard, Nottingham, Nottinghamshire

This is said by many to be the oldest pub in the country, dating to around 1189. It is a delightful building which has previously done service as a merchant house and watchmakers. Amongst its other claims to fame are the back rooms that are cut into the sandstone rock below Nottingham Castle, and the unique 'Ring O'Bull' game where you can see how much the ring has eroded the rock. Little nooks and crannies abound here and the history of not only the pub but also the surrounding area can be found in a museum next door.

THE CLACHAN INN

2 Main Street, Drymen, Glasgow, Scotland

The Clachan Inn is allegedly the oldest in Scotland and was once owned by Rob Roy's sister.

THE SKIRRID

Llanvihangel, Crucorney, near Abergavenny, South Wales

The Skirrid is the oldest pub in Wales, has an ancient studded front door, and is located near the base of Skirrid Fawr. It has a long and bloody history as in 1100 a man named James Crowther was hanged from a beam in the bar for stealing sheep. During the centuries since then over 1,800 more people were hanged in The Skirrid, which was also in use as the local courthouse. All of them met a swift ending by being hanged from the beam above the stairs, and the rope mark is clearly visible today as a gruesome reminder. It is thought that the last hanging took place in the late 17th century, also for stealing sheep.

The Inn has also had involvement in the Owain Glyndwr revolt against the rule of Henry IV, and the Monmouth Rebellion of the 17th century.

The Skirrid, Wales's oldest pub.

The Clachan Inn,
Scotland.

Ye Olde Trip
To Jerusalem,
England.

Beer was brewed by the ancient Egyptians, and it is the consensus of opinion that it had arrived in Britain by the Neolithic period. Over 2,000 years ago when the invading Roman army arrived here they tried to introduce wine by setting up Roman pubs called 'tabernae' (wine shops). The British were not impressed and preferred their beer, but the tabernae eventually gave birth to the idea of the alehouse. At that time beer was brewed everywhere, particularly in farms, and later even by religious bodies such as monasteries.

Various herbs were staple ingredients for flavouring and it was not until the 15th century that hops were imported into England, to be used as both a flavouring and preservative.

As brewing became ever more popular it was inevitable that the dreaded tax collectors would become aware, and as a result there has been a duty levied since 1188 when Henry II introduced the 'Saladin Tithe' to pay for the Crusades.

The magnificent Victorian gin palaces sprang up everywhere with the growth of the railroad, and this is how the large national brewers were able to expand - by following the rail network. There were far too many pubs at that time and they became more and more ornate to attract custom. The splendour of many of these opulent icons of the past can still be seen today but, sadly, they are fast disappearing as major national breweries cater more and more for young clientele.

THE SALTERSGATE INN

Saltersgate, Pickering, Yorkshire

Having a very picturesque setting on the North Yorkshire Moors, this historic inn is over 400 years old. Following the famous voyage by Captain Cook an unofficial voyage to follow it was planned here by Jack Lannerman.

Visitors will be amazed to know that the fire that crackles away in the cast iron range at The Saltersgate Inn has been doing so perpetually for over 200 years. You can read of the Saltersgate Inn Legend here that tells you the full story of this 'eternal fire'.

It is said that the devil himself will plague all the locality should the fire ever be allowed to go out.

WARREN HOUSE INN

Postbridge, Devon

The Warren House Inn has a fireplace at either end of its cosy bar, one of which has been kept continually alight since it was built in 1845. Prior to that the pub was located on the other side of the road and it is believed that a fire was also lit permanently there for at least 150 years. The reason behind this would have been for the benefit of tin miners working in the area, with peat being the traditional fuel. Although those days are long gone the tradition of keeping the fire alight lives on. Incidentally, this is also one of the highest pubs in England (1,545ft) and has no mains electricity or water.

WHITE CROSS HOTEL

Water Lane, Riverside, Richmond, Surrey

The White Cross Hotel is located on the site of the Observant Friars; a white cross being their insignia. As the River Thames floods regularly here a sign on the wall reads 'entrance at high tide', but the pub is perhaps better known as having fires beneath windows.

There were originally 3 of these fires positioned directly under windows although of the 2 in the flat above, one is now bricked up. The other is located in the bar. It is assumed that views of the river were wanted whilst sitting by a fire and hence the reason for this very rare arrangement.

BLACK BULL INN

Hall Lane, Mawdesley, Ormskirk, Merseyside

A spring water well, 40ft deep, lies under the floor of the Black Bull Inn. For the aforementioned fires on this page, the Black Bull Inn has an adequate instrument - an original black, 16lb poker about 4'6" long, and one of the biggest in the country. A quotation says of the poker: 'surely big enough to stoke and poke the fires of hell'.

MORRITT ARMS
Greta Bridge, Durham

The Morritt Arms is a former coaching inn which dates back to the 17th century and is named in honour of Charles Dickens who stayed here in 1838. He was on his way to start research for his famous book, Nicholas Nickleby, and in fact Greta Bridge is mentioned in the novel as the site of 'Dotheboys School'.

All around the walls of the splendid bar is a spectacular lengthy Dickensian mural painted in 1946 by J.V.Gilroy, who incidentally also has 6 of his old Guinness adverts on display here which he was more famous for.

BEEHIVE
Castlegate, Grantham, Lincolnshire

The most remarkable thing about this popular pub is that it has a living pub sign. It is in fact a hive full of bees, mounted in the centre of a lime tree and resident here since at least 1830 (and probably long before that). This makes it one of the oldest populations of bees in the world. A preservation order was put in place during the 1960's and is believed to be the only one in the country of this nature.

A 'hoody' (beekeeper) tends to the hive and the pub has the history of beehives displayed on its walls.

THE LAKESIDE INN

Marine Lake, Promenade, Southport, Merseyside

The measurements of this pub are just 22ft x 16ft and approximately 15ft high. If you should visit and wonder what the handles are halfway down the doors in the gents toilets - they were installed for the 7 dwarfs who visited the pub after appearing at the nearby theatre!

THE NUTSHELL

10 The Traverse, Bury St.Edmunds, Suffolk

Also widely acclaimed to be the tiniest of them all is The Nutshell that comes in at 15ft x 7ft 6in. It has to be said that The Nutshell is built on 3 floors and the measurements relate only to the ground floor. This amazing pub also boasts a mini fruit machine and jukebox, the smallest dart board and snooker table, and a wee Grandfather clock. Look out also for a 3 legged chicken, a left leg, and a mummified cat and mouse.

THE SIGNAL BOX

Coast Light Railway, Cleethorpes, Lincolnshire

Opened in 2006, the diminutive Signal Box has now laid claim to being not only the smallest pub in Britain but also the world. With a floor space of only 8ft x 8ft it certainly beats Sam's Bar in Colorado Springs, USA, which is 109sq.ft. It must be noted though that The Signal Box also has an outside drinking area. The Guinness Book of Records have their work cut out here.

DOVE PUBLIC HOUSE

19 Upper Mall, London W6

Many celebrity customers have been past visitors to the Dove Public House, and James Thomson (who wrote 'Rule Britannia') lodged and died here. Who knows where they all sat as the pub has the smallest bar in Britain - only 4ft 2in x 7ft 10in.

THE JOHN'S CROSS

Battle Road, near Robertsbridge, Sussex

The John's Cross Inn was once a recruiting office during the Napoleonic Wars. On a more up to date note the pub boasts very impressive floral displays outside and has been quoted in one gardening magazine as the 'hanging gardens of John's Cross'.

Another claim to fame here is that this is the only pub sign company in Britain actually situated on licensed premises (the studio is located at the back of the pub). The dining room is said to be the smallest dining room of any pub in the country at a measured size of 6ft 1in x 6ft 3in.

THE MINERVA

Nelson Street, Hull, Humberside

Built in 1831 on land reclaimed from the River Humber, The Minerva is a myriad of small rooms with one in particular being very, very small. The room in question is barely 4ft x 4ft and would be better described as a 'snug'.

EIGHT BELLS
Church Street, Chipping Campden, Gloucestershire

Of the 3 stone fireplaces at the Eight Bells, the gigantic one has a painting of the pub in summer. The heavy old oak beams with enormous timber supports indicate a great age, and this is verified by the glass covered section of floor that shows part of the secret passage which Roman Catholic Priests used to escape from the Roundheads.

THE WHITE HART
Worthgate Place, Canterbury, Kent

Reputedly haunted, The White Hart is built on the ruins of St.Mary's Church and is located only about a mile from Canterbury Cathedral. The cellar here was once the mortuary to the church and it still has the body chute in place. The small adjacent park was the graveyard where tombstones can still be seen along the wall. On the other side is an ancient Roman burial site.

OLDE FERRY BOAT INN
Holywell, near St.Ives, Cambridgeshire

This is one of the oldest inns in the country, with some people even saying it is the oldest. It can be dated back to at least 1068 with a disputed history that stretches back in time to the 6th century. The inn is reputedly haunted, particularly on the 17th March, by the ghost of Juliet Tewsley, a young lady who hanged herself from a nearby tree on that date in 1050 when her attentions were rejected by a local woodcutter. The Olde Ferry Boat Inn is built over her grave and a slab in the centre of the main bar marks her burial spot.

This ancient building has everything you would associate with such a great age and is well worth a visit, but not on 17th March!

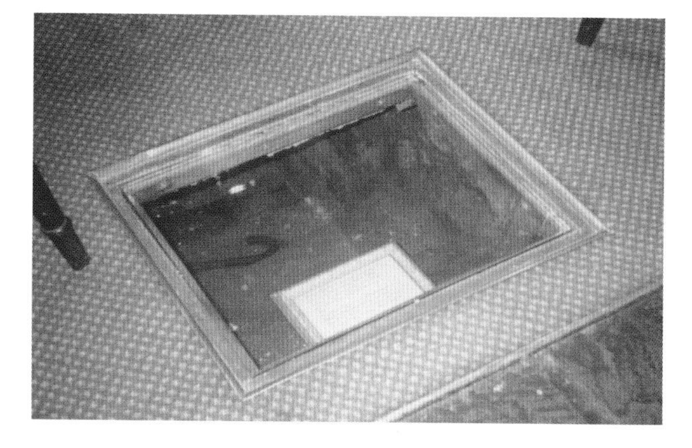

Secret underground passage at the Eight Bells.

THE WHITE BULL
Ribchester, Lancashire

A stuffed fox in 2 halves that appears to be jumping through the wall is a novelty that should raise a smile at the White Bull in Ribchester. The pub is situated in a former Roman town and there is certainly a lot of history here. The Tuscan entrance pillars have stood here for about 2,000 years.

THE CAT'S BACK
86 Point Pleasant, London SW18

This tiny pub has been described as 'eccentric with eccentric staff'.
It resembles a curiosity shop where visitors can admire - or ponder - the numerous odd and weird souvenirs that have been accrued here. African and Pacific island paintings, Indian chairs, and a host of bric-a-brac jostle for space in a myriad of fascinating clutter. The pub is named after a cat who disappeared but later returned.

BULL i'TH' THORN
Buxton, Derbyshire

Apart from its name there is a lot more of the bizarre to be found at the Bull i'th' Thorn. There are highly unusual carvings at the main entrance including one of a bull caught in a thornbush, another of some dogs chasing a rabbit, and an eagle with a freshly caught hare. The huge hall which dates from 1471 has a gigantic central beam which runs parallel with many smaller ones. Armour, 17th century German helmets, and even blunderbusses are on display.

THREE HORSESHOES
Bridge Street, Warham Village, Norfolk

Organs, pianos, musical boxes and much more can be seen at the wind-up gramaphone museum at the Three Horseshoes. There are even antique one-arm bandits in the pub itself.

TAFARN SINC PRESELI

Preseli, Rosebush, Clunderwen, Sir Benfro, West Wales

Constructed in 1876 when the railway was opened from Clunderwen to Rosebush, this was originally built and operated as a hotel under the name of the 'Precelly Hotel'. In 1992, in a bad state of repair, it was closed by the brewery and was subsequently bought by locals. Refurbished and re-named the Tafarn Sinc Preseli, it is now more like a home than a pub but this big zinc shed has traditional old world charm and values that everyone will appreciate.

Salt-cured hams hang from the beams, and a dresser, settles and lots of memorabilia jostle for space. Predominantly Welsh speaking here, visitors can enjoy panoramic breathtaking views all around; this is the highest licensed pub in Pembrokeshire.

No visit to the Tafarn Sinc Preseli would be complete without seeing the amazing reconditioned railway halt and platform here that is complete with life size dummies and sound effects.

THE HOLE IN THE WALL

5 Mepham Street, Waterloo, London SE1

Visitors to this pub will find that it is exactly what its name implies - a hole in the wall. The wall in question is a series of railway arches which are located just outside bustling Waterloo Station, and the pub is actually built into the railway viaduct.

Tired commuters can find solace here in the form of liquid refreshment, although the air is constantly punctuated with the sounds of trains rumbling on the tracks on the bridge overhead - which is the roof of the pub. The Hole in the Wall can be inspirational if you have yet to book your holidays for the year as the Eurostar makes its way overhead en-route to Paris!

WHITE HART INN
Nant-y-Ceisaid, Machen, South Wales

A plethora of ship's memorabilia greets visitors to the White Hart Inn which adds to the genuine feeling of being on a liner. In fact the panelling that can be seen throughout was salvaged from an ocean-going liner that was dismantled at nearby Newport Docks. The 'sea-legs' feeling will grow on you as you walk down the long narrow corridor and discover the hugely impressive bar - which should bring to mind the epic film Titanic - for those of you who have seen it.

A very pleasant unassuming pub found between Caerphilly and Newport, this is sure to appeal to sea-dogs everywhere.

THE OLDE SHIP
7 Main Street, Seahouses, Northumberland

Built in 1745, visitors to The Olde Ship will discover a veritable feast of nautical memorabilia. The items have been collected over a number of years and include ships wheels, figureheads, lifeboat oars, etc. There is even a museum upstairs with yet more artifacts. The pub has been in the same family since 1910.

Lindisfarne (Holy Island) can be visited via a causeway when the tide is out. It boasts the largest flock of wintering geese in Britain in addition to cormorants, whooper swans and other breeds. It is also possible to get a boat to Farne Islands which also has numerous colonies of birds, as well as endearing seals.

THE SEVERN BORE INN
Main Road, Minsterworth, Gloucestershire

Most of us will never see a truly huge tidal wave in this country but an equally spectacular and natural event - albeit on a much smaller scale - takes place frequently throughout the year on the River Severn.

A tidal wave known as The Severn Bore makes its way along the river and has been known to reach 2 metres in height. It travels at an average speed of 16 kilometres per hour, and the Severn Estuary is known to have the secong highest tide anywhere in the world. The difference between the highest and lowest tides on any given day can be over 14 metres.

The actual size of the bore can be affected by winds and freshwater levels which can influence both the height and time of the bore. On certain years major bores are anticipated and these draw large crowds of people from all over the country.

Probably the best vantage point of all to witness these exciting events is at The Severn Bore Inn at Minsterworth. It is located right on the banks of the River Severn and has a huge beer garden adjacent to the Severn which provides stunning views of these spectacular events.

PRINCE OF WALES
Kenfig, near Porthcawl, South Wales

Originally the medieval town hall and now the only remaining building in a town which has vanished into the sands, the Prince of Wales is part of an enigmatic tale that will both amaze and enchant you. The pub is located in Kenfig, near Porthcawl which is a popular Welsh seaside resort. Other than a scattering of farmhouses it is all that remains of the ancient city of Kenfig which was swallowed up by the sand dunes running down to the Bristol Channel. Amongst the structures forever lost to the sands was a hospital, church, and law courts. The church was built by Morgan Mwyn Mawr who was the founder of Glamorgan as far back as the year 520, and unbelievably Kenfig was once a superb commercial centre of trade. It boasted a river and seaport which were vital for trade links, and an impressive castle that had a gigantic moat.

The first calamity to befall Kenfig arose in 893 when it was almost destroyed by the Vikings. Up to 1402 it is believed to have been razed by fire no less than 8 times, but the greatest damage of all has always been inflicted by the shifting sands. Massive sandstorms were once very frequent, and even around 1450 the area was in dire straits with the castle almost overcome by the sands. The immense storm of 1607 finally put paid to what was left of Kenfig and buried almost without trace what little was left of it.

Amazingly the Prince of Wales survived, and ever since it has been subject to all manner of investigations to ascertain the compounds of its structure - which is believed to contain much of the local previously dreaded sand. The picture above illustrates the expanse of Kenfig Pool, with the Severn Channel further beyond the dunes. The tops of several structures swallowed up are clearly visible and this Atlantis type event has been keenly discussed in local towns for centuries.

The pub has played host to both the local Sunday School and parish council in upstairs rooms and could no doubt tell many a tale of the beleagured Kenfig history.

- biggest floating pub -

CHARTERS
Town Bridge, Peterborough, Cambridgeshire

Believed to be the largest continental barge in the country and probably the biggest floating pub, this boat is the 'Leendert-R', a riveted iron Dutch barge built in 1907 and working until 1990 carrying up to 616 tonnes of cargo. Now known as Charters it was sailed across to England and up the River Nene to the Town Bridge, Peterborough, and opened as a real ale bar in September 1991. At 176ft long it is certainly a sight to behold.

FERRY BOAT
North Fambridge, Essex

A peculiarity of this unpretentious, over 500 years old weatherboarded pub, is the fact that most of the building rests purely on a bed of reeds - which permit the old plaster and timber to move about in accordance with the local climate.

HALFWAY HOUSE

24 Fleshmarket Close, off the High Street, Edinburgh, Scotland

The Halfway House is a tiny establishment located at the foot of one of Edinburgh's atmospheric alleyways and is one of the smallest pubs in Scotland. It is actually a pub below a pub as it is completely situated under the main bar of the adjoining pub on steep, Fleshmarket Close.

Once the scene of gambling exploits of notorious rogue Deacon Brodie (a nearby pub is named after him), the Halfway House is full of character and characters. The curiously named Fleshmarket Close no doubt has many a dark secret it could tell.

The mysterious Fleshmarket Close with a partial view of one of Scotland's smallest pubs - the Halfway House.

THE LORD CREWE ARMS HOTEL

Blanchland, near Consett, Durham

The gigantic fireplace at The Lord Crewe Arms Hotel is believed to be the largest in the country and conceals a 'Priesthole' where Tom Forster (the leader of the local Jacobites) evaded capture by the King's forces during the uprising of 1715, although he later surrendered and was imprisoned. Once part of a 13th century monastery, The Lord Crewe Arms Hotel has many unusual features including a huge barrel vaulted crypt bar.

Blanchland, named for the 'white monks' who occupied the ruined abbey at its centre, is full of history which includes the pillaging by Scots in 1296. The gardens behind The Lord Crewe Arms Hotel were once the cloisters of the abbey, walked in solitude by the monks of Blanchland.

A most traditional inn, amongst other attractions is the resident ghost of a woman; not just any woman but Dorothy Forster, Lord Crewe's wife and the sister of Tom Forster. She rode to London in disguise as a servant, obtained duplicate keys, and aided her brother to escape prison and flee to France for his safety. She is now said to haunt the Bamburgh Room of The Lord Crewe Arms Hotel awaiting news of her brother.

THE YEW TREE INN

Cauldon Waterhouses, Stoke-On-Trent, Staffordshire

One of the most interesting collectors pubs in the country is the The Yew Tree Inn in Cauldon Waterhouses which appropriately has its namesake right in front of it - a giant Yew Tree. The location alone is unique, being situated between an enormous cement works and huge granite quarries, but the interior of the pub simply has to be seen. Such is the sheer oddity of this gem of a pub that it has been featured on Channel 4's Collectors Lot as inside you will find some of the most unusual items to be seen in any pub nationwide.

Working musical instruments (symphonions and polyphons) that are taller than a person, and are certainly something to behold, are merely a few of the many attractions here. Queen Victoria's stockings, pianolas, medieval wind instruments, valuable Staffordshire pottery, old firearms, a boneshaker, longcase clocks, a Jacobean 4-poster bed, an iron dog-carrier - the list is virtually endless.

Only a visit will enable true appreciation, but be prepared to spend some time here.

HIGHWAYMAN

Sourton, Devon

The Highwayman is one of those curiosity pubs that ensures several visits are required to truly satisfy inquisitive minds. The pub has a remarkable design that has been constantly bettered by over 40 years of input from the owners. The interior is a warren of flagstone floored intimate rooms with stuffed animals, intricately carved pews and other delightfully varied seating, plus quaint bow windows amongst much more that there is to admire. Also look out for 'Rita Jones Locker' which is an imitation sailing galleon that must be seen.

ALLENHEADS INN

Allenheads, Hexham, Northumberland

This amazing pub - courtesy of the renowned 'nutty' landlord - has every available space on the walls, ceilings, and it seems everywhere else covered with more than 5,000 collectibles ranging from a 4ft wooden chicken to long silenced musical instruments. There is no specific order here and visitors will find antique furniture in the dining room together with a plastic snake! It is truly an Aladdin's cave of memorabilia where the probability is that any item that comes into your head stands a good chance of being on display. Typewriters, stuffed animals, old radios, mangles, a ship's wheel, birdcages, shoes, an engine-room telegraph, even a vintage Rolls Royce is parked outside. The list is endless and the pub is one of Britain's top curiosity attractions that has to be visited at least once.

MILBURY'S

Beauworth, near Sheriton, Hampshire

A Bronze Age cemetery surrounds this pub which achieved a degree of fame in 1833 when a hoard of 6,000 silver coins was found there. On a more up to date note this popular pub has a 300 year old well (with a massive treadmill) which is 302ft deep. It is said that if you drop a coin into the spotlit shaft it would take about 8-10 seconds to reach the bottom, depending on the height of the fast flowing stream below.

Enormous treadmill, and (below) a barely visible shaft of light at the bottom of the 302ft well at Milbury's.

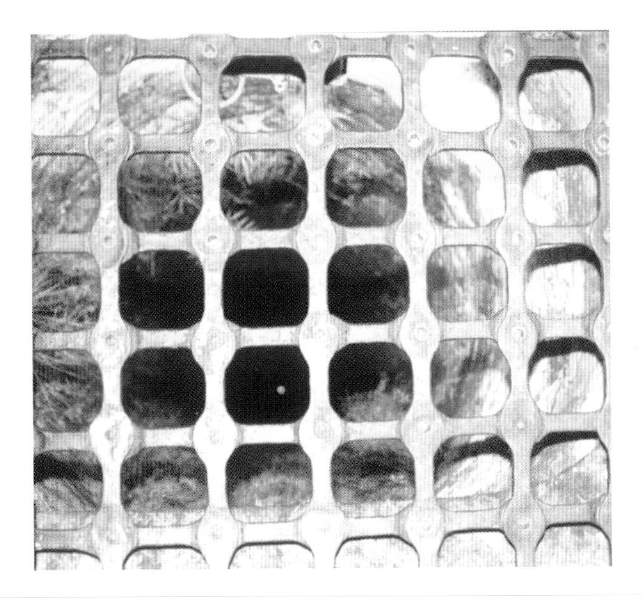

- a crypt and a corpse -

WATERGATES WINE BAR

11-13 Watergate Street, Chester, Cheshire

This bar and restaurant is set within what is said to be the oldest medieval crypt in England. Gothic archways, 3 long tunnels, and eerie lighting create a haunting, gloomy atmosphere in a building that dates back to 1120. It was in use as a morgue in the 1960's and there is said to be a ghost here. What is known is that a dead body was found under one of the floor flagstones in the 1800's, and it was then replaced and the flagstone dated.

THREE STAGS HEADS
Wardlow, Derbyshire

This small unpretentious, stone cottage pub has a tiny flagstoned parlour. The plates are home-made here - in addition to the food - as the barn is in use as a pottery workshop. Another curiosity is the petrified cat on display in a glass case. It was found during refurbishments and had evidently been bricked up alive centuries ago. It is believed it could have been the result of a macabre practice amongst local lead miners.

THE GEORGE INN
4 West Street, Lacock, Wiltshire

The tourist-magnet village of Lacock houses the Fox Talbot Museum of Photography, and also the ancient George Inn which dates from 1361. The centrepiece of this delightful inn is a gigantic fireplace which still boasts a roasting spit and a dog wheel. Extremely rare now, the dog wheel was a horrendous Tudor contraption that any animal lover would despise. It was essentially a small treadmill and is thought to have given rise to the expression - 'its a dog's life'.

The unfortunate canine who had to fit into this tiny thing was a special breed of dog known as a 'turnspit'. They were long-bodied and bandy-legged, no doubt due to the fact that they had to turn the spit that roasted the meat by the fire, in unbearable heat. Although this practice was stopped during Victorian times it was only because of the invention of a mechanical spit.

THE WHITE HART
82 Market Street, Ashby De La Zouch, Leicestershire

Once Dick Turpin's favourite drinking house, The White Hart has an old historic artesian well and a partly covered old bear pit. An enormous stuffed bear depicts what the scene may have looked like many years ago.

Old bear pit at The White Hart.

CROCKER'S FOLLY

24 Aberdeen Place, London NW8

Frank Crocker was a man with an eye for an opportunity and when he found out that the new railway terminus was to be constructed opposite, he knew his hotel would be a roaring success. The opulent Crown Hotel was subsequently built in a riot of Victorian splendour and with no expense spared. Over 50 types of marble were used and almost every part of the structure was encased in marble - columns, the bar counter, chimney-piece, even the walls. Added to this was an extravaganza of highly ornate plaster mouldings and reliefs, the finest quality woods including delicately carved mahogany, and an entrance hall befitting kings and queens.

Tragically, the railway terminus was constructed over half a mile away at Marylebone and Crocker, in total despair and by now almost penniless, hurled himself from an upstairs window.

The name of the pub now is indicative of man's folly in the single-minded pursuit of a goal. It is also however a splendid legacy for other generations to enjoy.

THE BLACK FRIAR

174 Queen Victoria Street, London EC4

This was built around 1875 on the old site of a 13th century Dominican Priory, The numerous illustrations and carvings of merry monks, which reflect its origins, were the inspirational work of Royal Academy sculptor Henry Poole.

PRINCE ALFRED

5a Formosa Street, Maida Vale, London W9

Little altered since it was built in 1863 this classic Victorian pub is sure to delight traditionalists. There are 5 bars, each unusually with their own street entrance. To move from bar to bar internally you have to stoop through tiny, waist-height doors in the partitions. Intended for access for the cleaners, they clearly illustrate the divisions that were apparent in Victorian society of bygone days. The original Private bar can be seen and even the Ladies bar complete with 'snob-screens', which were the order of the day to ensure a discreet level of privacy. The pub was actually named after Queen Victoria's second son who became Duke of Edinburgh in 1862 at the tender age of 18.

FREEMASONS ARMS

32 Downshire Hill, Hampstead, London NW3

Visitors will note a 'pell mell' court here which has survived from the original pub which was demolished after being found to be unsafe during extension work. The ancient game involved rolling a big wooden ball through iron hoops and was a form of croquet, but without the mallet.

There is also a London Skittle alley here in the Freemasons Arms cellar. The forerunner of tenpin bowling, it is played with 9 pins and involves throwing (not rolling) a cheese down a 21ft alley at the pins. The game is still played here on a regular basis.

THE SHERLOCK HOLMES
10-11 Northumberland Street, Westminster, London WC2

A pub themed on one of the most famous fictional characters in the world has to be a success and in 1957, following its return from a world tour, an entire exhibition that had been assembled for the Festival of Britain was purchased by a brewery whose aim was to create a London theme pub that would attract worldwide Sherlock Holmes enthusiasts.

The inn that had been known as The Northumberland Arms thus became The Sherlock Holmes, and with the aid and advice of Sir Arthur Conan Doyle's (Holmes's creator) family, the conversion was soon completed.

Adjacent to the restaurant in the pub there is a superb replica of Holmes and Watson's study which is brimming with authentic Victorian artifacts, and the whole place is a shrine to the legend that has arisen around this famous sleuth. Watson's old revolver is on display, as is the stuffed head of the Hound of the Baskervilles - plus an impressive collection of film and television stills, and much more.

Reproduction of Holmes study.

BEN CROUCHS TAVERN
77a Wells Street, London W1

The grave-robbing themed bar that is Ben Crouchs Tavern is actually based on a real character. Ben Crouch promoted boxing at the turn of the 1800's but was known as the 'king of the resurrectionists', probably because he had the monopoly on supplying cadavers to local hospitals for research and experiments. He was the son of a hospital caretaker and a well known London body-snatcher.

There are quite a few large gargoyles and shock-horror memorabilia scattered around this crazy apothecary styled pub in addition to a gruesome depiction of Ben Crouch himself. The toilets are quite scary and you feel as if you have mistakenly entered a crypt. This is also the meeting place of the London Vampyre Group who congregate here on the second Thursday of every month.

Devilish setting for a pint in London.

Count the gargoyles at Ben Crouchs Tavern.

ROYAL OAK
200 The Broadway, Cardiff, South Wales

Hardly altered since well before the turn of the century this remarkable pub even has its own professional boxing gym. The pub itself is a sporting shrine, with boxing in particular taking pride of place. Pictures of famous boxers from all over the world jostle with a magnificent range of memorabilia for wall space and there is hardly a square inch of flock wallpaper to be seen. 'Peerless' Jim Driscoll's career is recorded on the walls of the bar and he was once himself a Cardiff licensee.

Worth seeing at the Royal Oak are the intricate stained glass screens behind the bar which have shielded the windows for over a hundred years.

THE EAGLE
Bene't Street, Cambridge, Cambridgeshire

Many claims to fame here including the fact that this pub was once the headquarters of notorious swindler John Morlock who headed the Rutland Club in the 18th century. The high ceiling here has been untouched for many years so that the numerous signatures worked in with candle smoke and lipstick (done by British and American airmen during the war) are not covered up. The Eagle was a favourite watering hole for the famous Nobel Prize winning scientists Francis Crick and James Watson. In February 1953 Francis Crick announced in the pub that the clever scientists had unravelled the secret of life - they had discovered the structure of DNA.

Part Two

- USA -

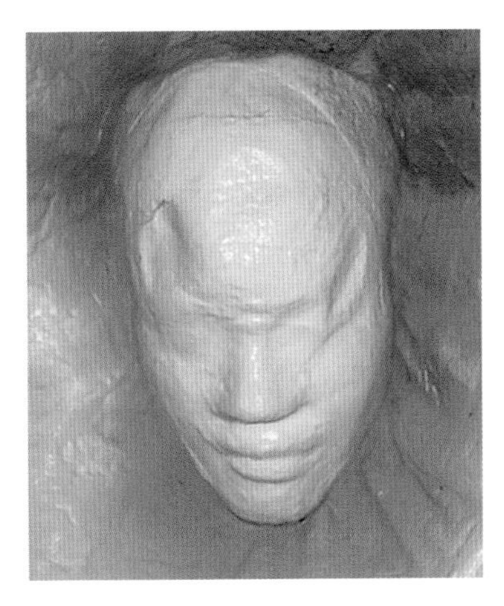

Things may not be quite what they seem at the Korova Milk Bar - page 71.

McSorley's, the famous New York City,
East 7th Street institution.

McSORLEY'S
15 East 7th Street ,
New York City, New York

If you can handle the unpredictable weather then a visit to the time capsule that is known as McSorley's is highly recommended. Opened in 1854 (although some say 1862), the place has hundreds of old photographs on the walls which customers have brought in through the decades, and this pub has lived through everything including the 1863 Draft Riots, and both World Wars. McSorley's did not admit women until 1970 and was one of the last male-only bastions in the city. Even today it still has the appearance of a Wild West saloon with swing-doors, sawdust covered floors, and a long wooden counter as a bar.

The pub once used 4 different soup bowls instead of a cash register; one each for pennies, nickels, dimes and quarters. Visitors may wonder what the dust and fluff covered things are hanging from a light fitting. They are in fact turkey wishbones. The tradition dates back to World War I when soldiers who were going to war would each hang a wishbone there. The soldiers who came back removed their wishbones, and the number still there is testament to those who never returned.

EAGOR'S BAR AND GRILL
1018 Hermosa Avenue,
Hermosa Beach, California

Located in Hermosa Beach next door to the Comedy and Magic Club, this is a great family horror themed bar and restaurant where furniture levitates and items suspend or move in mid-air. The Halloween themed room was constructed by a Disney set designer to illustrate a Hollywood horror scene and is extremely realistic. Props and memorabilia from many famous shock-horror movies can be seen in glass cases - all in a haunted house setting.

THE SPACE ROOM LOUNGE
4800 SE Hawthorne Boulevard, Portland, Oregon

There are many bizarre places to visit in Portland including the Alien Museum but nothing will prepare you for the creativeness of The Space Room Lounge. It has been likened to entering a discotheque on the top floor of a UFO, such is its effect on visitors. This wacky retro bar is a cross between Star Trek and The Jetsons, with flying saucers everywhere and space scenes painted throughout. Neon painted murals, 1950's light fixtures, and rocket fuel cocktails combine to make you feel as if you are in the middle of a Super Nova starburst.

It has never been updated and the twee magic of original television space programmes and series from the 1950's can be felt here. Worth a visit just to hear the oldies such as Star Man and Monster Mash on the jukebox.

Madonna Inn, the famous Californian motel and watering hole that is so 'over the top' you have to see it.

KOROVA MILK BAR
200 Avenue A (between 12th and 13th Street), New York City, New York

The Korova Milk Bar; is it a vision of the future, or simply a bizarre production of the depths of its creator's mind? This was partially designed with the futuristic drug den in Stanley Kubrick's famous film 'A Clockwork Orange' in mind. Weird films and strangely shaped mannequins can be quite disconcerting for the first time visitor but it is certainly an experience. The party nights are quite famous.

MADONNA INN
100 Madonna Road, San Luis Obispo, California

This has been a California coastal landmark for over 50 years. The motel has over 100 different themed rooms to sleep the night away in such as the Antique Cars room, Bridal Falls, Sweepstakes, and even Sir Walter Raleigh room. The watering hole here is called the Silver Bar. Hand carved wood and rock have been used throughout, and The Flintstones 'Bedrock' would be a more appropriate name for it.

Eccentric, or simply a bizarre mind-boggling vision of the future at the Korova Milk Bar.

CAVEMAN BAR-BQ & STEAK HOUSE

26880 Rochester Road, Richland, Missouri

Visiting here requires you to first find the place, secondly negotiate the dirt roads in a beaten-up courtesy van which picks you up, and thirdly ascend in an elevator which takes you through the limestone bluff wall up to the restaurant which is inside a cave - 50ft above the road! The decor is crazy and hilarious, sometimes defying adequate description, and the owners are justly proud of their weird caveman attraction. Once inside the Caveman Bar-BQ & Steak House you can stroll over to the deck area which overhangs the river. You are 100ft up from the river, and the cave even has its own waterfalls and fountains.

David Hughes, the former Wichita policeman turned farmer who rediscovered the cave, decided it would be a good place to have a restaurant. The transformation took over 4 years and 160 tons of rock was removed from the cave using not much more than shovels, wheelbarrows, and a jackhammer. Air conditioning and dehumidifiers were installed, fish-stocked fountains and waterfalls were added, and seating, tables and finishing touches made. The opening night attracted 300 customers, and in the first 8 months 35,000 people were served. The visitors book shows that people have travelled from all over the world for the unique experience offered by this innovative attraction.

The surroundings of the cave are remarkably cool. The dehumidifier pumps out 9lbs of water every hour and there is a constant temperature of 69F. An earthy interior greets you from the elevator, but soft lighting and antique furnishings create a pleasant and inviting atmosphere. You are surrounded by natural rock formations, and of course the eccentric decorations that together with the unusual location have helped make this establishment famous.

The cave has a somewhat chequered history and this is not the first time it has been used for entertaining. During the 1920's prohibition era it was in use as a dance hall (or speakeasy as they were known) and a natural rock ledge at the back was where people sat whilst waiting for the opportunity of a dance. In those days visitors did not have the luxury of an elevator and instead had to scale an old ladder to enter the cave. Around about that time a man named Ed Steckle constructed a resort complex below the cave, and alongside the Gasconade River. It is said that 50 construction workers worked for just 50 cents an hour each on this project, but when Steckle died the resort and cave sat empty for a number of years. The cave is also said to have had other uses from time to time.

Whatever its past, the Caveman Bar-BQ & Steak House of today is a unique eating experience. Huge burgers, steaks and ribs, are some of the attractions here - and of course the Caveman experience.

The hard way to enter the Caveman Bar-BQ & Steakhouse - or simply take the elevator.

THE TRACTOR BAR

Route 41, Mount Nebo, West Virginia

This local landmark was originally a retail store for tractor parts and tools, and the farm tradition has continued since its conversion into a tractor themed bar. Visitors love to be photographed with the antique tractor that sits in the bar here and the pub has been voted in the top dozen 'weirdest and wildest' bars in America by GQ magazine. One look around the place and its easy to understand why. On one wall is a huge pair of women's underwear that were made from feed sacks, whilst the various t-shirts on sale give a fair indication of what to expect at the rowdy live music events, and even the occasional 'mashed-potato' wrestling matches (don't ask) that are held here.

The bar has a simple philosophy which is written on a wooden sign - 'A farmer needs a new tractor every 15 years, but he needs a beer every day'. Hmm . . .

SAM'S BAR

22 N.Tejon Street, Colorado Springs, Colorado

With plenty of competition throughout the world - and in particular from Britain where there is now a pub measuring just 8ft x 8ft in floorspace - Sam's Bar is striving to maintain its grip on being famous as the smallest pub in the world. Opened in 2002, this Colorado Springs establishment has a bar area of just 109sq.ft. As there is obviously much kudos to be gained from the accolade of 'world's smallest pub' - not to mention the countless visitors who descend on the place to have their photograph taken there - it is thought that Sam's will fight tooth and nail to retain their accolade.

Small pubs will always have an appeal to curiosity seekers who simply have to see the place, but is there any real money to be earned from miniscule drinking places? Anyway, I'm just off to take a delivery from the brewery at my latest venture - a pub in a phone box!

Will the t-shirts at Sam's Bar have to be redesigned to say the world's second smallest bar?

Part Three

- REST OF WORLD -

The result of one too many at Pasha's Cafe Bar? - page 82.

CABBAGES & CONDOMS

Tanarai Road, Chiang Rai, Thailand

Right in the middle of nowhere is the Cabbages & Condoms bar and restaurant which is an avid supporter of family planning. The owner, Khun Mechai Viravaidya (a former Thai Minister of Health), is something of a local celebrity and became renowned for visiting brothels and other places of illicit entertainment dishing out free condoms. Because of this a condom is now referred to locally as a 'Mechai'. At this small village in the north of Thailand you will stumble across his Cabbages & Condoms establishment. Cabbages are a staple part of the diet in Thailand and the condoms bit of the name is obviously due to his benevolent nature in dishing out the johnnies. Such is the popularity of this unusual establishment - which it must be said serves excellent food - that it has now mushroomed into a thriving chain with outlets throughout Thailand. They all raise funds for the 'Population & Community Development Association', the country's family planning program.

The main restaurant is the one located in Bangkok in a garden setting which is reached via a pleasant lane. Here all diners get a condom instead of an after-dinner mint and there are amusing signs and references to condoms and family planning throughout, including a huge copy of the famous 'Mona Lisa' holding a packet of pills. The walls are awash with posters and ornamentation extolling the virtues of safe-sex and a sign states that 'condoms should be available as freely as vegetables in a market'.

The gift shop next door has condom shaped key chains, flowers, and all manner of other phallic related objects, or perhaps you could buy a copy of 'From Condoms to Cabbages' - the life story of Mechai, Thailand's remarkable Mr Condom.

The topic of conversation after dinner and drinks at Cabbages & Condoms is family planning.

Religion and alcohol fuse together at Het Elfde Gebod.

HET ELFDE GEBOD

Torfbrug 10, 2000 Antwerp, Belgium

Better stocked with more religious artefacts than any church or cathedral you have seen, Het Elfde Gebod (translated in Flemish as the 11th Commandment, which seems to be eat, drink, and be merry) is a riot of colour with statues galore. Angels, Saints, pictures of Christ, and church memorabilia everywhere. Situated behind Antwerp Cathedral you can also expect to hear organ music whilst supping a pint of beer. Just tell the wife your popping to church every night. Think she will believe you? You haven't got a prayer.

RED SEA STAR
near North Beach, Eilat, Israel

Housed in a trio of welded steel tanks that are anchored by concrete, the Red Sea Star is submerged 20ft under water and is reputedly the world's only underwater bar and restaurant. Named after the sea in which it sits, The Red Sea Star enables you to feel part of the sea in a 'dry diving' experience that is quite unique. Breathtaking views through the 62 panoramic windows allows you to see hundreds of exotic sea creatures and a colourful coral garden. This exclusive underwater bar is quite spectacular by night when you can enjoy the rare sight of the beautiful aquatic world in a softly lit setting, but without disturbing the creatures.

The Red Sea Star is reached by crossing a 200ft long bridge which connects it to the shore. The entry pavilion is just above sea level and has a lounge, coffee bar and kitchen. Drinkers or diners (or both) then descend 2 levels to the bar and dining areas. It is quite a surreal experience to be enjoying your meal when an unexpected dining companion appears a foot or so away from you, but its only a diver taking a closer look at what your having for afters.

Since opening, the media coverage that the Red Sea Star has received throughout the world is quite exceptional. The unique concept that it is based upon and the fact that it is a 'green' project make it all the more remarkable as it blends in so effortlessly with its aquatic neighbours.

Off the shore of Eilat sits the Red Sea Star, a complex construction that was made with 6,000 tons of steel and concrete. It was designed by architect Sefi Kiryaty, and the steel sections were fabricated in the north of Israel in 1995 before being transported in convoy trucks to the port of Eilat where they were welded together to form 3 massive structural units. The load cell has 2 primary functions, one of which is to create a mass at the base of the structure to prevent it from floating to the surface, and the other is to keep the structure level in relation to the surface of the sea. The seabed had to be levelled before the first section was set in place. This section weighed 200 tons even before it was filled with concrete.

The restaurant and bar section weighs approximately 110 tons, and the floor is star shaped to maximise interior space and provide window seats for almost every visitor. The windows weighed 12 tons and had to be imported from Japan as there were few manufacturers in the world who could produce the special design that could enable the windows to withstand the enormous pressure of the seawater bearing on them. The third section, which is above sea level, weighs about 120 tons. This houses the entrance lobby, coffee shop, auditorium and kitchens. It is said that the sight of the completed structure when towed by tugs from the port to its final location was quite astonishing. Over 4,000 tons of concrete was poured into the base under water to sink the structure into the seabed, and then it was anchored to 34 huge piles which were driven through the base into the seabed to a depth of 15 metres. This amazing structure can even withstand earthquakes.

PASHA'S CAFE BAR

Centrum Rezydent, ul. Bohaterow Monte Cassino 53, Sopot, Poland

The hugely distorted building that is Pasha's Cafe Bar resembles something you would expect to see at a funfair, but it is actually one of Sopot's top hangouts for the trendy in-crowd by night, and curious visitors and tourists by day. Most people would struggle to name a famous Polish architect, and now we know the reason why.

Human settlement in Sopot dates back about 2,500 years and this was once a small fishing village in the 13th century. The baths and spas of this fashionable health resort attracted the wealthy and aristocratic set to Sopot in the 17th and 18th centuries, then during the 19th and 20th centuries, Sopot (which was then part of the Prussian partition of Poland) attracted Europe's ruling classes. It became part of the Free City of Gdan'sk under the Treaty of Versailles and Adolf Hitler even spent a week here in 1939 while the German Army marched towards Warsaw.

These days Sopot is the in-place to be. There are numerous trendy shops, restaurants and bars, and the nightlife is reputed to be the best that Poland has to offer.

BAR SODA

Hotel Victoria Ship, 4F, 5-16 Kosone-machi, Nagasaki, Japan

Permanently moored in Nagasaki, there are loads of rooms to explore on this floating wonderland of a boat including the Bar Soda. Surrounded by windows on either side, you have perfect views of the water and the shore. The drinks are crazy and include specialities such as the Gorilla Nipple, which is a cocktail. Even the odd sailor calls in here from time to time and it is one of Japan's most unusual bars.

BLUE BAR

3-10 Wakamatsu Building, BFI Nakasu, Fukuoka, Japan

The name says everything here as everything is blue. Only the Japanese could go to these extremes as any length of time spent here could leave you feeling that you've been cloned with the flashing blue light from an ambulance.

Enter the Blue Bar to see blue ceilings, blue walls, blue floors, and blue lights. Add to that blue cocktails made with blue curacao and served by luminous blue bar staff. The effect is quite startling and you feel as if you've been on some psychedelic trip. The only white things seen in here are the palms of my hands and once I've been to the toilet I'm going to wash them with the blue soap here - then dry them with the blue towel.

Not an optical illusion, just the bizarre Pasha's Cafe Bar viewed from different angles.

Get high on the drinks but the plane stays put.

LETKA TU 104 - AIRPLANE BAR
Legionarska Ul, Olomouc, Czech Republic

Brought here in 1975 to be converted into a restaurant for the communist elite and their companions, this is now a late night bar in the uninviting centre of Olomouc. The entrance is a steel staircase towards the rear of the plane and you have to wait by a locked steel cage until the bar person answers your ring on the doorbell. Once inside it is like stepping back into the 70's and 80's. The original aircraft seats of this Russian Tupelov aeroplane remain and everything else is equally as dated. Only the television and gambling machines appear to be less than 20 years old.

The novelty of this plane bar would be the best reason to visit as the sign prohibiting firearms is none too inviting. Towards the cockpit area there is even a dance floor where you can amusingly watch the locals doing a Czech version of the twist to some 70's or 80's classic that's belting out of the jukebox.

The plus point here that many people would like is the fact that Letka TU 104 is open till 7 in the morning, way after Olomouc's other watering holes have closed. I for one would rather give up drink completely than run the risk of meeting some communist drunk hellbent on continuing the revolution on a grounded aircraft.

AUGUSTINERBRAU KLOSTER MULLN
Augustinergasse 4, Salzburg, Austria

This must be one of the largest beerhalls in the world and is almost a mini-town under one roof. From the outside you could not imagine what you will encounter within as the street entrance is small and almost unmarked. Once you have climbed a few flights of stairs and enter, you may think you have mistakenly gone into a shopping centre. Not only can you bring your own food, if you wish, there is even a row of small shops here including a butchers and bakers. On into the drinking area and there are several massive baroque rooms with enormously high ceilings. The customers are a mix of seasoned drinkers, families, and even a grandmother here and there - all drinking from litre steins. They also have unusual little copper devices filled with warm water that allows you to warm your beer to the correct drinking temperature. The beer here is served direct from oak barrels and is quite inexpensive.

Augustinerbrau Kloster Mulln is situated in part of a real monastery in the old suburb of Mulln and this is the only religious establishment in Austria which still brews. A stein or 2 of beer and some of those delicious German sausages makes for a very pleasant few hours. Everyone else here has the same idea it appears.

LE CERCUEIL
10-12 Rue des Harengs, Brussels, Belgium

Cercueil is the French word for coffin and you'll find plenty of them here. The tables are coffins, the bar has coffins, and there are even coffin lids on the walls. Dark and atmospheric, this has been here over 30 years and is one of the oldest horror bars in Europe, if not the world, and they take frightening the life out of you very seriously. Belgian humour is at its best here and although this looks a distinctly grim place from the outside you will be goggle-eyed when you step in from the long dark hall. There are not only waitresses on roller blades here but also everything to do with death in a morgue-like setting. Here you drink out of ceramic skull mugs whilst sat around a coffin table, gaze at the sombre purple and velvet decor, and blink in the ultra-violet lighting which is designed to bring out the customers pallor. The funeral theme is not melancholic but this is no ordinary bar.

The house specialities here are potent cocktails such as Sperme du Demon (Demon's Semen) and Urine de Cadavre (Corpse Urine). The pub has one large room and a smaller overflow room for when it is busy, and it always is. Candles everywhere (so don't wear that nylon jacket), and the sombre music of Gregorian chants, funeral marches, and the 5th Symphony of Mozart; what more could any graveyard enthusiast want.

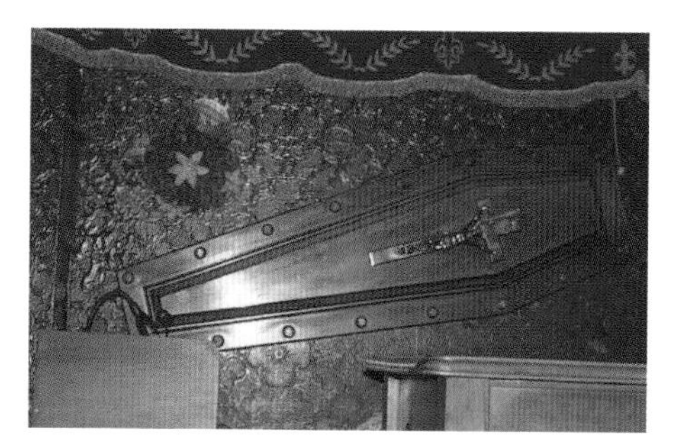

You'll be coffin up for the drinks at Le Cercueil, one of Europe's oldest horror pubs.

Don't be late for your funeral at Le Cercueil.

Everything is made of ice at Absolut Ice Bar including the glasses.

ABSOLUT ICE BAR
Vasaplan 4, Stockholm, Sweden

You can find the Absolut Ice Bar, the world's first permanent ice bar, just off the main lobby of the Nordic Sea Hotel in Stockholm. The interior is maintained at a crisp -5 degrees centigrade all year round and everything here is made of ice; bar, tables, and even the glasses.

When you arrive you pay a cover charge for clothing and a choice of drink, and then get kitted out by an Ice Bar employee with a silver cape-parka, mittens, and protective footwear if required. After you have entered the first door you have to wait until it is closed before entering the second. This is to keep the cold inside as much as possible. The bar offers a choice of drinks including cocktails made with Absolut vodkas, and they are all served in the special hollow ice glasses which are made of pure, clear ice from the Torne River in northern Sweden. Of course you have to be a swift drinker to prevent your drink icing up.

The Ice Bar, which opened in 2002, is now one of Sweden's most celebrated watering holes and is a must for any visitor with a list of sights to see. The concept for the ice glasses was developed at the Ice Hotel in northern Sweden in 1995. The first glasses were hand cut from pristine blocks of ice from the Torne River and proved so popular that a factory and production line was established to produce the frozen glasses. Over a million of these glasses are used at the Ice Bar and Ice Hotel every year. The carefully cut blocks that line the walls of the Ice Bar were also shipped in from the Torne River area.

Red noses, frostbite, and a chill that does your best friend no good at all are memories you can take away from the Absolut Ice Bar. Real good fun and must be experienced at least once. Readers may also be interested to know that there is also an Absolut Ice Bar in London, England.

MUSEUM HR GIGER BAR
Chateau St.Germain, Gruyeres, Switzerland

An image springs to mind when you enter the cavernous structure that is the Museum HR Giger Bar, and that image is a scene from the original - and best - Alien film by Ridley Scott; the one where actor John Hurt drops into the bowels of an alien spacecraft and a creature emerges from a 'pod' and attaches itself to his helmet visor. The sheer immensity and skeletal-like structure of the bowels of that spacecraft must surely have been the inspiration for this bar, and indeed they were as H.R.Giger - a local artist from Gruyeres in Switzerland - was a designer on all of the Alien sci-fi horror films.

The design and construction of the Giger Bar in Gruyeres, which opened in April 2003, took 3 years and it is hoped that it will be the prototype for Giger Bars all over the world. There is already another one operating in Chur, Switzerland, and a third was opened at The Limelight in New York City but was closed when The Limelight shut down. It is rumoured that an employee made off with one of the $30,000 chairs when the bar closed and it has never been recovered.

The ceiling structure at Museum HR Giger Bar in Gruyeres was cast in fire-retardant fibreglass and the complexity of the work is astounding. Double arches of vertebrae crisscross the vaulted ceiling and there are many other quite astonishing features to be seen there.

Giger received an Academy Award for the original Alien movie and his artistic expression has frequently been called 'biomechanoid'. It is said that he, more than anyone else, has given the most profound insights into the depths of the human mind, in particular with his sometimes frightening visions of prenatal and perinatal depictions that are often intermingled with what some would regard as grotesque distortions of what we perceive as normal. Giger, and his work in many other fields other than film, can be adequately described as a genius. He will be remembered by generations to come.

An alien world awaits you at the Museum HR Giger Bar in Gruyeres.

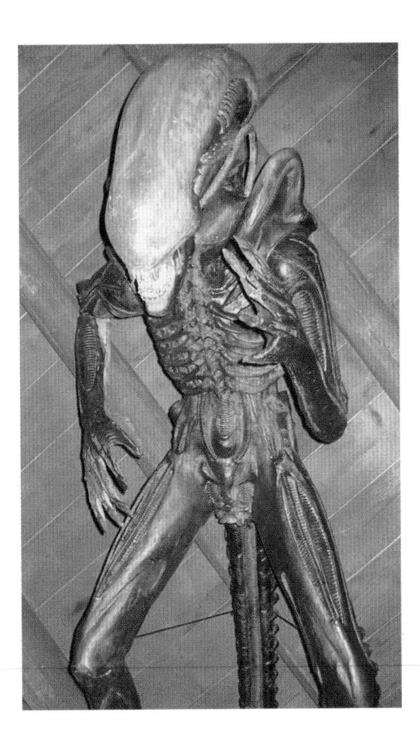

'1975'
Monet Street, Beirut, Lebanon

At the lower end of Monet Street, which is the heart and soul of Beirut's now vibrant nightlife, is the '1975' bar - so named after the Lebanese civil war and bizzarely themed to recapture the atmosphere. Bearded waiters with dogtags - in combat gear and helmets - serve your drinks in a war-torn atmosphere that has tank shells on the stairs, wartime graffiti on the walls, and a huge effigy of a masked militiaman climbing up a pillar over the bar.
A musician strums the 'Oud', which is a traditional Arabic lute, and plays nostalgic songs that were aired over radio continuously to calm people during periods of heavy bombardment. The new generation of young people who sit around the bar and upper lounge, under sandbagged walls and camouflage netting, are interrupted from conversation when a 'Mulhak' (newsflash) that was taped during the war to announce heavy shelling is played. The customers even puff on military style metallic Arguileh hookah waterpipes, and eat a cheese spread on 'Kaak', which is a traditional Lebanese hard-crust sesame bread that can be stored for a long time and was considered a staple food during the war.

The bar was established to remind the Lebanese people, and the world, that the war is not yet over. In 2006 it was far from over and '1975' bar may be yet another casualty of the seemingly endless troubles in the region.

Beirut, as the capital of the Lebanon, has a dramatic position as it juts into the sea and has mountains rising behind it. It stands on the site of an old settlement and 5,000 years ago it was an affluent town on the Canaanite and Phoenician coast. The name can be dated back to the early 14th century B.C. when it was then called Berytus before becoming a Roman Colony. Earthquake and fire struck in 551 A.D. and in the next century it fell into the hands of the Crusaders where it remained until conquered by the Mamlukes in 1291. Ottoman rule commenced in 1516 and lasted for centuries until the defeat of the Turks in the First World War. In 1943 Lebanon gained its independence. The troubles surrounding Beirut and the Lebanon over more recent decades is not a subject to be discussed here, particularly in view of more recent troubles, and it is hoped that the area can find a peace that is befitting a land that has some of the most wondrous sights and history to enjoy.

Important remains covering the Ottoman, Mamluke, Crusader, Byzantine, Roman, Persian, and other periods in Beirut's history have been discovered - and continue to be discovered. There are many superb buildings and ancient mosques that relate much about the history and life and times of old Beirut.

On the western tip of Beirut stands its most famous landmark, Pigeon Rocks, which is a huge formation that seemingly guards the coast.

Help yourself at Piatiy Okean.

PIATIY OKEAN
Marksistskaya 20, Moscow, Russia

What a good idea. There is no bar counter at this friendly Moscow pub, just beer taps that are mounted at each table (picture above). Customers have to pour the beer themselves and the bill is calculated later for every 0.1 litre consumed. All the beer is delivered in special fermentation tanks from the pubs microbrewery that is located in the outskirts of Moscow. Light Unfiltered and Dark Unfiltered are the popular brews.

SHTOLNYA
Zatsepsky Val, 6/13, Moscow, Russia

Mining was once a huge industry in Russia and even today it still plays a major role in the Russian economy. This pub, Shtolnya (meaning Mine Gallery), is a spooky semi dark cellar decked out as a mine. Huge timber columns and brick walls full of authentic mining memorabilia can be seen, with everything from helmets, lamps, shovels, picks and air-hammers. Well worth seeing should you take a 'Red' holiday.

JUNGLE JUNCTION
Bovu Island, Zambezi River, Zambia

Believe it or not the little village of 20 or so huts on sub-tropical Bovu Island has its own pub - well, more of a bar really. This island is a sort of no-mans land with the Botswana Customs on one side of the Zambezi and the Zambian Customs on the other. It is only a few hundred metres long and is covered in dense forest. As you approach the village through the low hanging vegetation the woven sides of the bamboo huts come into view. There is a labyrinth of rat-runs that cut through the undergrowth and connect different parts of the island. Without these it would take hours to hack your way through even a short stretch of forest. All the huts here have mosquito nets and wooden beds that are hand-made on the island. If the huts are full there is also a campsite where you can cook on charcoal, and you bring your own tent or hire one here. The dinner cowbell in the evening rouses you from whatever you are doing and afterwards you can relax in the candle glow of the thatched, open-sided bar - which is the heart and soul of the island, and even has a crazy collection of hats.

Bovu Island is a truly magical place and from the comfort of the bar you can watch the hippos wallowing in the Zambezi. Inquisitive monkeys frequently come up to the bar, or you can sometimes be quite amused watching them gathering some freshly fallen fruit. A bar from paradise!

THE PONDEROSA BAR
974 Glenshane Road, Dungiven, Co Derry, Ireland

This famous Irish pub is quite unique and is mentioned in numerous books including the award winning novel 'Harry's Game', written by Gerald Seymour. There are many peculiarities here such as the fact that the pub is totally self sufficient. They have their own turf bank for fuel, a personal electricity generator, and their water supply comes from a spring well in the mountainside. It is also noted as Ireland's highest pub at 1,000ft above sea level.

The Ponderosa was once a simple little farmhouse at the highest point on the mountain road between Belfast and Londonderry. Today, a wide highway crosses the Glenshane Pass, and the pub overlooks Glenshane Adventure Forest. If anyone is feeling energetic enough to climb the Glenshane Pass under their own steam then the pub will award them a special certificate. Congratulations, you are now a member of the exclusive '1,000ft club'.

The Glenshane Pass is on the main Derry to Belfast route and cuts through the special area of conservation that is the Sperrin Mountains in Northern Ireland. The 'Sperrins', as they are known, are a range of hills and the region stretches from south of County Londonderry to the west of Lough Neagh in County Tyrone. One of the most beautiful areas in Northern Ireland, the Pass in particular has some severe bad weather during winter.

DE KOE
Marnixstraat 381, 1016XR Amsterdam, Holland

Tiny and eccentric, this 2 floor pub/restaurant has a tiled mural outside of a cow wearing a scarf, which should give you a fair idea of the decoration to be found inside. De Koe means 'The Cow', and one bar has a car racing set glued upside down to the ceiling and a collection of barbie dolls hanging on chains. Of the many quirky things to be found here the most bizarre must be the collage behind the bar made from photographs of raw meat and naked women.

WUNDERBAR
19 London Street, Lyttelton, New Zealand

Wunderbar is a real oddity and is one of the strangest and most unique bars in New Zealand. People travel from far and wide to see the collection of infamous dolls heads that the pub has; this is in addition to a huge collection of other weird items that are scattered throughout the building.

book orders & suggestions

We hope you have enjoyed reading this book and will want to purchase other titles of Strangest Books. Please see the back cover for a brief description of other titles currently available in this series.

Our books can be purchased from all good book shops and a broad selection of other retailers. Alternatively, you may wish to visit our website where excerpts and images from other titles can be viewed free of charge, and books may be ordered direct.

We are always interested in hearing from readers with any comments or suggestions. If you would like to contact us please use the relevant e-mail link below.

e-mail direct

bookorders@strangestbooks.co.uk

suggestions@strangestbooks.co.uk

or visit our website at:

http://www.strangestbooks.co.uk